Listen to Them

Charles A. Faulkner

Listen to Them

Charles A. Faulkner

CITIOFBOOKS, INC.
3736 Eubank NE Suite A1
Albuquerque, NM 87111-3579
www.citiofbooks.com
Hotline: 1 (877) 389-2759
Fax: 1 (505) 930-7244

Ordering Information:
Quantity sales. Special discounts are available on quantity purchases by corporations, associations, and others. For details, contact the publisher at the address above.

Printed in the United States of America.
ISBN-13:   Paperback   978-1-963209-82-2
                      eBook   978-1-963209-83-9

Library of Congress Control Number: 2024904382

To my friends at KTLA Channel 5, whose oft-expressed feeelings of love, affection and concerns for animals-their own as well as those they come across in the news they report on-are akin to my own love, affection, and concern for all animals

Maybe those folks are listening to them!

Table Of Contents

INTRODUCTION

Communication!

For we humans communication is an essential. It is an essential between husbands and wives. It is an essential between the men on earth and the space ship in space. It is an essential between a boxer in the center of the ring and the handler in the corner, the coach on the sideline and the quarterback on the field, parents in the home and their children in their care. Communication is essential, so much so that when communication is lacking, the results are confusion, misunderstanding, goals lost, opportunities missed. Poor communication can have disasterous results.

So communication is essential between each pair of each entity. But for each singular side of every entity pair, the most valuable asset of communication is the component known as listening, when coupled with its attendant component, hearing. Listen, listen and you might hear the door opening into the thought pattern. Listen and you might grasp the intention through the body language, for communication progresses best when listening is utilized and embraced by both sides of each entity pair. This is never more true than when dealing with relatively tame animals or domesticated pets. Such was the case in the first story in this writing. I listened and heard the oppossum's plea through her body language. My wife listened and heard the oppossum's mental plea.

Here are three conversations. Listen to them

Conversation #1: Ya done good girl

This a true story about an encounter with two oppossums.
This is the conversations with those oppossums.
Listen to them.
Conversation #2: Three questions
This is the true story about the life of one of my cats.

1

This is about the conversations with my cat.
Listen to them.
Conversation #3: Dichotomy
This is a conversation.
This conversation speaks true.
Listen to them.
The validity of the dialogues presented here is open to debate. The veracity of the events is not.
Listen to them.

PART 1:
YA DONE GOOD, GIRL

Looking out the back door into my backyard. I happened to notice a tint baby possum slowly, shakily negotiating the short grass in the yard. From time to time, it would be one of the larger ones, The next moment, one of my cars came along the pathway. It spotted the little fellow, stopped, and watched it for a moment. She then moved over to the little guy, sniffed it, then pounced on it, and then began to play with it as though it were a little ball, tossing it up into the air. I quickly hurried out into the yard calling to my wife and shooting that cat away. We recovered the possum and put it in a box along with some water. At this point, the possum apparently had taken refuge in its well-known catatonic state. In the box, it lay on its side, not moving. From the moment my cat had pounced on it till I shooed my cat away, my cat had not had time to harm the little fellow and only tossed it into the air once, before I rescued it. As I mentioned the small possum for the next several minutes, it suddenly snapped out of it lethargy after about fifteen minutes. Our intentions were to take the little guy to animal control a few days hence, when they opened on Wednesday.

Monday, April 1, 2013
Early evening

Looking out my front door, I noticed my cats all looking in the same direction. Turning to see what they were looking at, I saw a large opossum slowly moving in my direction along the front of my house. The cats had him surrounded. As he reached the side of my front steps, he laboriously came on to the step. I called my wife. He hesitated a moment. Then he slowly continued moving in our direction, even climbing another step higher toward us. I thought, That's odd. At our home here, I'd seen many possums- in our front yard, in our backyard, along the side of the house. And always they ran as fast as they could to get away from us. They never move toward people.

Suddenly, my wife said, "He's hurt." As I looked at him, I could see that the side of his face was bruised. His back also had a large bruise. He continued to look at us. Then my wife said, "He wants us to help him." She moved toward the possum. He turned and ever so slowly began to move away. But then he looked around at us again and stopped on the step. Ellie shooed the cats away while I went to get a carrier from the backyard. Then she remembered that in the cardboard box sitting on the top step was a small carrier. She got it out and shooed the possum into it. She brought it to the backyard, where we transferred him into a larger carrier with the intent to take them both to animal control, which would not be open until Wednesday. We decided to call our vet to find out what we could feed the small possum till Wednesday. They directed us to an animal hospital. We called that hospital, spoke to a lady, and told her about both possums. She said she would stop by after she got off work and take both animals back to the hospital. We said we'd wait for her. Later that evening, Ellie went to the yard to check on the two possums. When she returned, she said the larger possum had died. I went to the yard and looked into the carrier. The large possum showed no signs of life. He was unmoving, and his eyes were partially open and had a glazed look. The day before, when the little possum had gone into that catatonic state, he looked as though he were asleep. This big possum had an entirely different look. I was sure he was dead. I also noticed a circular area about the size of a quarter on his belly area, which was reddish and showed signs of having bled. This poor creature had suffered body trauma before he reached us. A slight movement at the rear of the carrier caught my attention. Before I had put the possum into the carrier, I had put newspaper on the floor of the carrier. The possum, after entering the carrier, had bunched up at the rear of the cage. Now the paper was quivering slightly from time to time. I attributed that to the slight breeze that was blowing. But just to be sure, I went and got a flashlight and shone it on the possum and then the paper of the rear of the carrier. I was surprised to see three tiny baby possums moving around back there. That adult possum was female and had been giving birth when she died. I was stunned. I was also suddenly very sad. Realizing this new scenario brought tears to my eyes. She must have been very, very concerned for her babies. Hurting as much as she was, I believe she held herself together until they were in a safe place. Then she died. I looked down at the dead mother possum. I looked at the three baby possums. It was then I knew what the epitaph of the mother should be, and through my tears, I spoke out loud to her but in a soft voice and said, "Ya done good, girl. Ya done good. You got your babies to us, and so now they have a chance. Rest in peace. You done good, girl. You done good."

When the lady from the animal hospital arrived later the evening, we told her what had happened. We took her to the carrier. When we looked inside, we saw that the three baby possums had moved from the rear of the dead mother up into the hair of the dead mother. One of them had crawled up all the way into the hair on the head of the mother. Even as we watched, the other two were slowly making their way in that direction.

The lady from the animal hospital said that possums usually have about a dozen babies. We then disassembled the carrier. The lady reached in and turned the body of the dead mother over. The lady said, "Hear that sound?" I listened, and I could hear a ragged squealing. The lady said, "That's the babies calling for their mother..."

She began pulling them off one by one and put them into the carrier she brought with her. One of the babies was dead, so she left it. She left taking all the young possums plus the first one we had rescued the day before. She said they would be taken care of either at the hospital where she worked or at her home.

Later in the house, Ellie was very quiet. She turned to me and said, "Why am I crying over a possum?" I told her, "For the same reason I am. The mother tried to protect her babies. She got them to us. Then she died. She done good. I just hope that before she died, she knew that they were safe. I hope she knew that."

PS: A few days after, my wife told me when the possum was on our front step looking at us, she, Ellie, could hear it in her own brain asking for help but not in normal English words. She said she couldn't explain it, but she could understand what the possum was saying.

PART 2:
THREE QUESTIONS

HAVING A PET IS A BEAUTIFUL THING.................................

LOSING A PET IS A HURTING THING......................................

I HURT.........................

I CRY............................

I SPEAK.......................

Last week there were nine cats at my house and the house was full, because Shasta was in it. Today there are eight cats at my house, and the house is empty because Shasta is not in it and I miss him. I really really miss him.

The value and worth and regard I hold for all my remaining Cats combined, do not come close to the value, worth, and regard I hold for Shasta. That is not an indictment of the inadequaies of my other cats, but rather an affirmation of the depth of affection I hold for Shasta. After all, the other cats are just cats. Shasta, Shasta was special!! Very special!!

Let me tell you how very special he was. But first…why am I writing this paper?? I'll tell you; for two reasons. First, it is therapy for me. And second; I have an obligation to Shasta.

First, my therapy;
The depth of my affection for Shasta has, in turn, determined the depth of my pain at his loss. I hurt!! And the pain I feel can only be assuaged by formulating the memories of him into verbal concepts which I can then project onto paper which then serves as a screen that displays the life of Shasta. That, for me, is the therapy I need, to deal with the pain I feel, and, over time, the pain should become less intense. But, for now I hurt!!!!!!

Second, my obligation.

I have an obligation to Shasta an obligation to establish a verbal memorial to him, because he deserves it. Shasta's intellectual acuity needs to be recognized, for it allowed him to accomplish a note-worthy feat in the furtherance of animal-to-human-to-animal connectedness. He probed and probed until he succeeded in breaching the wall of human awareness. This allowed him to function in that arena in a way that was human-istic. When we expressed our affection for him, he was then able to reciprocate in kind, letting us know that the feeling was mutual. Most cats' reaction to our expressions of affection was decidely self-centered. They tended to preen, and strut and say, "tell me more.", Actions that said "my owner likes me. I must be doing something right". Shasta, on the other hand, responded in A way that said your action pleased him too. His action said "Thank you. Right back at-cha___humanistic-like.

Long before Shasta became ill and passed, I anticipated the effect it was going to have on me. Years before, while he was Completely healthy, there were moments when I would look at him, after sharing some moment of joy with him, I would quietly think, "it's going to hurt when I lose you." And my eyes would brim with tears. But then I would shake it off, and tear my mind Away from that inevitability and substitute the mother of all States of denial Shasta was going to live forever!!

If only...............

That early anticipation was accurate. It was going to hurt. It Hurts! I hurt!!!!! .... I hurt for Shasta.

I observed Shasta for ten years.
From Shasta's actions, I deduced his thinking.
From Shasta's thinking, I deduced his intentions.
From Shasta's intentions, I deduced his words.

Pretty Boy

Shasta

Mr. Special

CHAPTER I
THIS LAND IS MY LAND

In 2002, kitty brought Shasta, love bug, and grey-boy as part of a three cat package gift. Shasta and grey-boy were brothers. Love-bug was a 'cousin' so to speak. They were all about 5 years old. We kept them in one room of the house, allowing them out into the kitchen to eat. We allowed them to roam the house during the day as long as we were at home. Each night we would lock them in their room. After one week, we let them roam free at night with free access to the whole house. At first, they would return on their own to sleep in their own room. About the third night of that second week, we awoke to find all three had climbed onto our bed to sleep. The second night that this happened, Shasta, as I was talking to him face to face, gently pushed his forehead against mine. I was mildly surprised by this gesture but at the same time, surprisingly pleased as well. I realized that it was a friendly reaching out on his part. Although at the time I didn't realize it, that was the start of our connectedness. In the ten years he lived with me, either he or I would initiate this gesture, and always, the other would respond to it.

The three cats were confined to the house for about the first three weeks. Then they were allowed to go out and investigate the back yard, where I had about six stray cats already in the yard. Shasta and the other two roamed the yard, getting familiar with everything. By then I had decided to shorten the name of one of them, "lovebug" to "bug". Kitty had given them their names but i, knowing that at times it was necessary to search for my cats who were new to these environs, and I refuse to one night walk down a dark alley searching calling "here lovebug, here lovebug", and have some dodo thinking they're hearing someone whose Viagra has gone off on them!

After about the first 3 days of Shasta roaming the yard, I noticed that I would not see my other 6 cats out there. THEN ABOUT THE 4th DAY, I SAW SHASTA AGRESSIVELY CHASE TWO OF MY SIX STRAYS OUT OF THE YARD. I stopped him. The next day at feeding time, I didn't see any of my strays. Shortly, they appeared, coming from the front yard and the alley. When Shasta would show up, they would leave. I didn't like that. Those 6 were my cats. Shasta was new to me. Though I didn't like this situation, I was committed to accepting Shasta. The 6 cats, I learned, were living under my neighbor's house 3 doors down. I tried every day to discourage Shasta from this activity. After about 2 weeks of chasing the six away, Shasta finally relented and left them alone. Gradually the six again took up quarters in my backyard.

Chasing Strays

CHAPTER II
SHASTA CONFRONTS THE FLAME

Shasta was a tough cat and after learning to leave my other cats alone, he chased away all other stray cats that attempted to enter our yard. He had several fights on our property. I don't like to see or hear any cat fight, but they do happen. Whenever I would hear the sound of a cat fight I would immediately hurry to the location and break it up. Always my first concern was, was one of my cats being abused!?

About 2004 Shasta was in his prime and was more than able to hold his own in a cat fight. Usually when I would arrive at the site of a battle Shasta would be chasing some cat out of the yard. But from time to time a cat would show up that was as tough as he was. On occasion, upon hearing the ugly sound of a vicious cat fight and rushing to the location, I would find Shasta and some cat locked in a battle to the death, neither wanting to back down. I always restrained Shasta and chased the other cat away.

One day I broke up a fight between Shasta and a reddish color cat. The cat ran out of the yard. The next day that cat was back. Shasta wasn't around so I chased the cat out of the yard. The following day Shasta again got in a fight with this cat. When I got to the back door; I saw them facing off and Shasta slowly advancing on the red cat which was slowly backing up. I chased him away. Later that day, talking to my neighbor I learned she liked that red stray cat and was feeding it. The next day I witnessed something I had never seen before, ever nor have I seen it since.

Hearing the sound of a cat fight, I hurried to the back door. When I got there the fight had stopped, but as I watched, Shasta and the red cat were facing each other, but only Shasta was making a sound. He was emitting that soft varying pitch, threatening yowl cats make when they are about to fight. But only he was making the sound as he, in painful slow motion, advanced on the red cat. The red cat was motionless, sitting there facing Shasta. It was as if Shasta had hypnotized that cat. Relentlessly, in super slow motion, Shasta advanced, his head slightly bowed until he was right in the face of the red cat, who sat as though petrified. Then, astonishingly Shasta raised his head and licked the red cat right above his right eye once, twice, three times. I was afraid the red cat was going to sink his teeth into Shasta's throat. Still I didn't move. After the third lick, Shasta slowly drew his head back from the face of the red cat. They looked into each other's eyes, then, still in slow motion, Shasta turned to his left and slowly walked away. The red cat remained frozen for about another 15 or 20 seconds. Then it too came slowly into the yard. I couldn't believe what I had just seen. It was as if Shasta, through that ritual, had told the red cat "buddy I see you are almost as tough as I am and I kind-a like you. So I'm going to allow you into the family. But you just remember this—I am the boss and I could wipe you out. But we'll strike a truce". They never fought each other again. The red cat, who I named 'flame', became a part of the yard family and he took on the job of running outside stray cats out of the yard whenever Shasta wasn't around, and he was as ferocious in that job as Shasta was.

CHAPTER III
SEARCHING, SEARCHING

As strange as it may sound, the longer Shasta lived with me the more convinced I became that he was bored with being a cat!! Sensing something in his attitude and demeanor, it appeared to me that his mind was probing constantly probing, trying to comprehend something that was ostensibly beyond his ken, his feline mental boundaries, his feline awareness. That is, I sensed that he had minimum interest in behaving like cats do in general.

Most animals, I believe, regard humans as just another animal. I don't think they give any thought to this regard, but their animal instincts for humans are the same as their instincts for any other animal. That is, they relate to humans as if we were contesting for food and water, and shelter for survival.

However, when we take on a domesticated animal as our pet, that animal eventually subjugates its natural instincts for survival to our proffered gestures of security and care. But always that animal sees us as just another animal, though kinder. They never realize that there is a wall between animal awareness and human awareness. Then comes along a few animals that are able to sense or learn of the two awarenesses. When such an animal turns up, he becomes curious about the difference and he attempts to investigate it. If some one of we humans is fortunate enough to be adequately observant, and that animal and that human cross paths, the result is a special combination. I am that human, and Shasta was such an animal, and his intellectual acuity enabled him to bridge the wall to human awareness seven times, and on two of those occasions he initiated an action himself and those two occasions showed he clearly understood the close relationship he and I had. This was brought home to me because one of those actions he repeated with me on three separate occasions. The second action he repeated twice.

I continued to get the impression that his mind was restlessly seeking what ever was there that would challenge his intellect. I began to feel that his mind was hungry for such a challenge, and I felt regret that I knew not how to feed that hunger, nor did I have the time it would take to explore my suspicion. What made me feel these things? It was the way he would sometimes look at me. Intently. Maintaining his gaze on me for unusually long, though brief periods of about 5 to 10 seconds before looking away. He often seemed pre-occupied, distant, as if thinking. Sometimes Shasta would wander away from the house, seemingly exploring the neighbor-hood. I always lost track of him when he would get 5 or 6 houses down on the other side of the street. He engaged in this practice over a period of many months. One day as I was returning home in my car, I spotted Shasta in our block, sitting on the doorstep of one of my neighbors, 6 doors down, just nonchalantly looking around. I slowed and looked at him. He looked nonchalantly back at me. I drove on home. Shortly after I arrived at the house, Shasta casually strolled in. On several occasions over a period of many months I would see Shasta at that house but at different points of the property. I knew the lady who lived there, and she knew Shasta so I was not concerned. And then there was the time when once again as I was returning home in my car, coming from the opposite end of my block, I spotted Shasta around the corner of my neighbor's house seven doors down sitting on the grass just nonchalantly looking around, observing, and thinking.

Shasta rarely played as the other cats did, but he was warm and cuddly to us humans. I did teach him simple things like the word eat, which he knew meant food was ready, and out, which he knew meant go outside. But all the cats knew those words. However, there was one word only Shasta responded to, and that word was hug

Whenever I wanted to pick Shasta up and hug him I would say the words "Shasta hug, Shasta hug". He never failed to respond to that call but he chose the manner in which to respond. Once I gave that call, no matter where he was in the room with me, whether behind me, in front of me, beside me, once I said those words, he would casually move behind me then walk toward me until he was standing between my legs. There he would stop and wait. I would then bend down and pick him up and hug him. Once picked up, he would be semi-relaxed in my arms for about 30 seconds. After that, he would start moving to be put down. I never held him past his 30 second fidget point. On occasion he might give you 45 seconds of a relaxed armful before the fidget point was reached. Sometimes when I picked Shasta up, wanting him to share with me the pleasure of this ritual, I would hold him and, in my best, imitated baby talk voice-goo-goo sound, my chin just above his head, I would say "good boy Shasta, good boy," leaving the 'd' off "good". And every time I babbled thusly, he always took his cue and would tilt his head back until the top of his head would gently touch the bottom of my chin, and he would maintain that contact for about 5 to 10 seconds. For the period of that head-to-chin contact there was a mutual Shasta-charles-Shasta sharing of pleasure and bonding, that only an animal lover can truly appreciate. Shasta and I had connection.

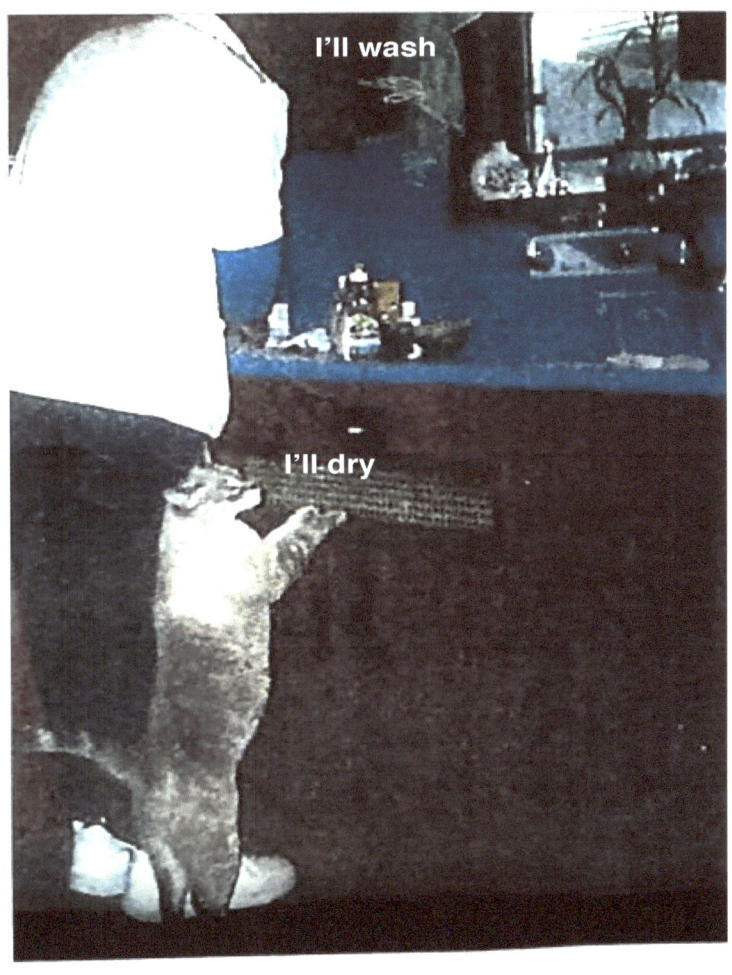

17

CHAPTER IV
A PEOPLE CAT

Shasta was a 'people' cat. He coveted being petted. He sought interaction with humans. Whenever visitors showed up at my house, all the cats always made themselves scarce. They did not want to be around strangers and would go hide themselves. Shasta was different. When strangers arrived in the house, Shasta would keep a distance away at first. But if the guests remained in the house for perhaps 10-15 minutes, Shasta would slowly come within our midst, evaluate the reaction, and if the guest seemed friendly, Shasta would carefully approach the stranger and allow himself to be petted, as long as I or my wife was present. He seemed to relish the attention.

There are many aspects of Shasta which mark him as special, but one of the most remarkable was his willingness to endure the dang-erous propensities of the "little people" children ages 2---6. These people, when they appear on the scene, bring noise and chaos, so much so, that animals, dogs and cats flee in a panic to distance themselves from the little darlings, and find someplace to hide. Shasta also would move away when the little ones would appear, but not in a panic. He would still be seen hanging around the outer reaches of whatever the location was. After a period of time, maybe ten minutes, he would cautiously move toward these little darlings. Once they spotted him they would move toward him. Their parents would caution them to be gentle with Shasta. Shasta would not run as they approached this second time. When they would touch him, he would patiently endure their rough petting, unless it became too rough. Then he would carefully move away, until they calmed down. If they controlled themselves he would once again allow himself to endure their presence and their touch. Not one of all my other cats ever did that. They would keep away and remain hidden until the little people left.

It was incredible that this cat refused to panic... This cat that was strong, and Healthy, and fast, and tough, would stand his ground when the little people, who were covered in chaos would charge him. He just refused to panic. Shasta was special!!

On a couple of occasions, after one of the little people seated himself on a sofa, Shasta would even come to the sofa, jump up on it and curl up right next to the child and allow the child to pet him. This always delighted the child, and even Shasta seemed content with this arrangement. Somehow, he seemed to know that this arrangement was of value to the little human, so he sacrificed his own feline independence, even risked his own safety to give the child pleasure. Another example of this propensity (I was just reminded of this scenario from the past by my wife's grand daughter, who is now 14 years old). At the time of this occurrence she was about 4 years old.

One night she was allowed to stay overnight at our home, sleeping on the sofa. When she retired that night and was about to doze off, she recalls Shasta jumped up on the sofa and curled up right next to her and allowed her to pet him. When she went to sleep, he was still there. When she awoke next morning, he was on the floor eating his breakfast. Now, at 14, she says she enjoys that recollection.

Oh yes, Shasta was special, the lady kitty, who had Shasta from birth through the first five years of his life said that she and her family members all marked Shasta as special. They said he just seemed different. One of her friends, after being around Shasta for a while remarked that "that cat was more than just a cat". And he was right. Shasta was just different. As has been noted, whenever his gaze would fall on me and hold for several seconds, it was always as if he were contemplating something, thinking. The other cats whenever they looked at me it was as if they were saying "wha…?…Wha?…Wha…?…Aint it time to eat yet?" And still others look at me and don't have a clue, seemingly totally mystified at the sight of me. Their face seems to say "what are you anyway? By the way, aint it time for my snack?" After all, they are just cats. But I love 'em all.

SHASTA LOVES PEOPLE!!!

Kitty and Shasta

CHAPTER V
"HE AINT A HEAVY, HE'S MY BROTHER"

The third example of shasta venturing into the area of human awareness came about 2 years ago. At the time I just thought it was a cute example of shasta reacting to a situation similar to the way we humans would have reacted. At the time I wasn't in touch with the "big picture" and so was not aware of how significant his reaction really was

Shasta had a brother, blue boy, who was owned by my neighbor, mary-lou. Since our two yards were adjacent, her cats were often in my yard and mine in her's. Between my house and the neighbor on the other side of me was a fence. This fence served as a launching pad for all my cats whenever they wished to visit the roof of this neighbor. They would climb up on my fence and then propel themselves up on my neighbor's roof. I tried to discourage this practice every chance I got but to no avail.

One day when I was working in my back yard, some of my cats were hanging out there, tending to their cat business. Blue-boy came into the yard. He looked around, then decided to check out the view from above. He leapt up on the fence, then launched himself up on the neighbor's roof. I had been observing him all along, and when his feet touched that roof, I yelled at him "blue-boy down". He froze, looking back at me for about 5 seconds. Then he quickly reversed himself, went back to the fence and down to the ground and quickly hurried on out of the yard. Shasta, who was present there in the yard, took note of his going as he looked toward the retreating blue-boy. Then he swung his gaze to me and held for about 3 seconds, then back to blue-boy, then again back to me. Then he nonchalantly walked toward me. When he got within about 5 feet of me, he lost a series of yowls at me, maybe 6 of them in number. I had the distinct impression he was giving me 'what for' for yelling at his brother. I felt called upon to issue an apology to Shasta for yelling at his brother, which I did. Now I know you all think I made this all up. But now get this; the very next day the exact same scenario repeated itself. Again, I ordered blue-boy down from that same roof. As he left Shasta again, he was in the yard witnessing it all, and again after observing in turn his brother, then me, he again walked over to me and let loose with that same set of sounds!!! This time I didn't apologize but instead told Shasta "Well tell your brother to keep off the roof!!!"

At the time I only thought it was cute, Shasta's action. I did note it signified his intelligence. But not until recently, after starting to see the whole picture, did I begin to grasp what Shasta was doing. Cats do not take up for their family members! Well, excepting mother cats for their brood, and that's only in the 'protect-from-harm' mode. This does not apply here. Shasta and blue-boy were only brothers, and there was no threat of harm to blue-boy, so Shasta's objection was only verbal not physical. Shasta was an animal trying to function in human awareness, and he was succeeding.

I believe that Shasta's first foray into the arena of human aware-ness began when he first began to butt heads with kitty, the lady who first owned him. When she first told me about this event, I assumed she had taught this to him. Later, as I recalled how she described how this came about, I realized it was Shasta who first initiated this action. I believe that his intelligence caused him to understand that the driving force of the feline anatomy and the human anatomy was the head. I believe that his instincts were leading him to sense that by engaging these extremities of the two species, he was symbolically conjoining the boundaries of feline awareness and human aware-ness. As you may recall, he was quick to bring that practice into our, his and my, relationship. He was testing to see if he and I were on the same wavelength. Next, he accepted my chin-to-his head contact as a pleasant physical connectedness, which encouraged further excursions. I suspect he was noting my responses to his probing and began sensing our kinship in the animal-to-human-to animal connectedness.

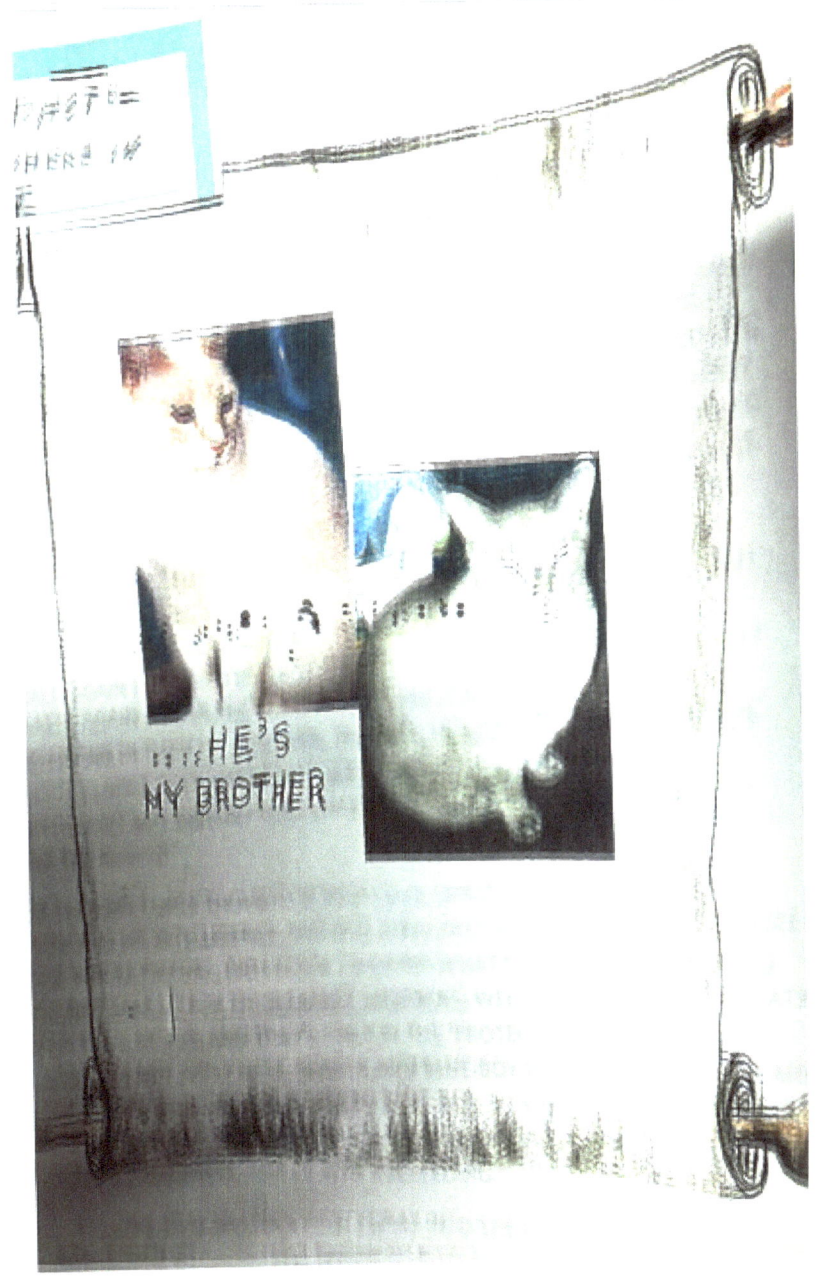

CHAPTER VI
A FAST LEARNER

Shasta was a fast learner. He quickly picked up on cues that were meant to indicate that a particular response from him was expected, and he always responded. Case in point; Whenever any of the cats got doused with rain and came indoors, they naturally shook themselves to divest themselves of the wet. Eventually I got the idea of grabbing a towel and reaching for the cat to dry him off. They would have none of it, tearing themselves out of my hands and running away for dear life. But not Shasta. He allowed it, standing patiently while I rubbed the towel all over him. The next time the cats got soaked, the previous scenario again played itself out. Shasta was the only one to permit this.

The third time Shasta got soaked, I grabbed the towel but I didn't approach him. He looked, saw the towel and casually walked toward me and stopped in front of me, waiting. I would tell him to lie down, which he did. I would dry him on one side and, having taught him the command, tell him to "roll over", which he would do, allowing me to dry his other side. Always he was patient throughout this procedure.

And then there were the times when I was about to feed Shasta in the kitchen. He would be sitting there waiting for me to put his plate of food down, when sometimes I'd have to leave the kitchen briefly because of some need in another room. I'd tell Shasta "just wait Shasta, just wait". And after being gone from the kitchen for a few minutes, I'd return and nine times out of ten, Shasta would still be at the exact same spot I left him in, waiting. I would put his food down, and then he would eat.

CHAPTER VII
SHASTA REACHES OUT

Shasta had been with us for almost a year when I began to take note of one of his many sleeping patterns. After having gone to bed, sometimes I would awaken in the middle of the night and discover Shasta cuddled up asleep against my leg. Other nights he would be cuddled up against my wife's leg. Some nights after seeing this, I would go back to sleep, only to wake up again one or two hours later, and find Shasta asleep in the space between the two pillows. Sometimes he would be so relaxed that he'd be asleep on his back. It was always a joy to see that because it meant that he was completely at ease. Then there were other nights I'd awaken to find Shasta sleeping with his head on my pillow. That was always a beautiful sight. He looked so at ease, so totally at peace. I would look at him at those times and enjoy the sight for a time. But then again, it was at times such as this that that painful thought would crawl across my mind, "it's going to hurt when I lose you". But as always, I would push the thought aside. Then I would turn over so as not to have my face breathing the same air as he. I loved my cat but not that much.

And then came Shasta's fifth foray into human awareness. Sometimes when he would be sleeping between the two pillows, he'd awaken. Then I'd awaken to find him lying there looking at my face. As I watched him, his eyes would be moving across my face. Then I got a pleasant surprise as he reached his paw out and gently placed it on my face. The gesture brought two sensations. One was the joy in experiencing such tenderness from him. But secondly, always his claws would be out and though the gesture was tender, the light prick of his claws marred the gesture. As soon as I would feel the claws, I always pulled my face away, out of an abundance of caution. His claws are too close to my eyes and whereas he may intend no harm, a sudden unexpected movement could result in his claws pricking my eyes. So, always I withdrew my face. This scenario was repeated over the years about 3 more times.

In the interim, Shasta shifted his choice of sleeping areas from one location to another, sometimes on the bed, sometimes not. And occasionally he repeated the scenario with his paw. I didn't know it at the time but looking back, Shasta was processing his incoming information. It was now about 3 years after Shasta first put his paw with claws on my face. Now I was about to experience his 5th foray into human awareness.

Once again, he was on the bed looking at my face. Shortly thereafter, he reached his paw out and placed it on my cheek as he had done so many times before. When his paw touched my cheek, I was prepared to allow it to remain there for about 3 seconds as I had always done, when suddenly it hit me. His paw was on my cheek, but not his claws!!! They were sheathed. You cannot imagine my surprise. I did not move my face away this time. I simply enjoyed the elation this realization and touch brought. I smiled. He let his paw remain on my face for about 6—10 seconds. Then he removed it. He was still looking at my face after about another 5 seconds he again placed his paw, claws sheathed, back on my face. I was ecstatic! I softly said the words to him which he had come to recognize as signifying my thorough satisfaction with him…:" good boy Shasta, good boy". Again, after about 5—10 seconds he withdrew his paw. Then, after looking at my face for about another 5 seconds, he jumped off the bed.

No, I don't his thought processes led him to understand the need for that change. But I do think his instinct, operating on the human awareness side, caused him to feel that change was appropriate for that moment. This cat was special.

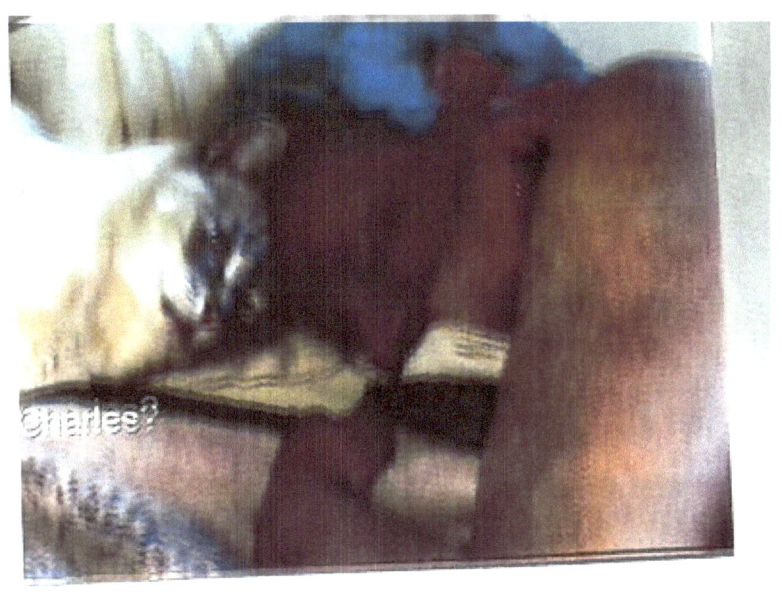

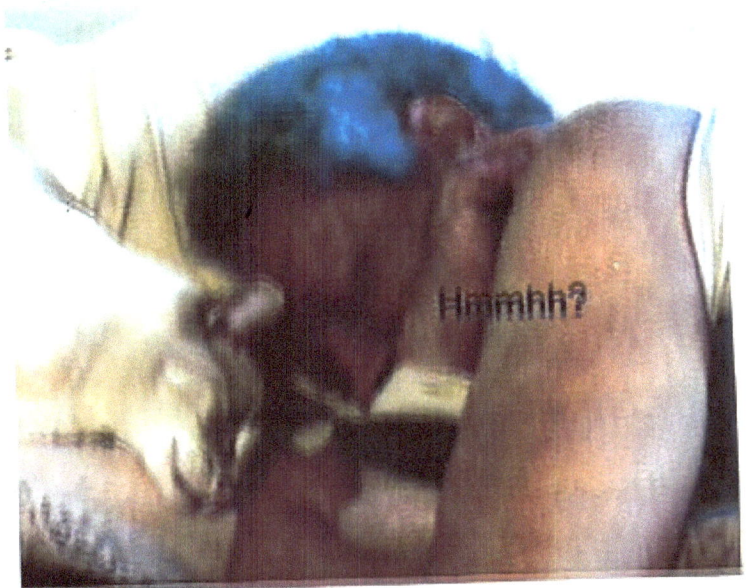

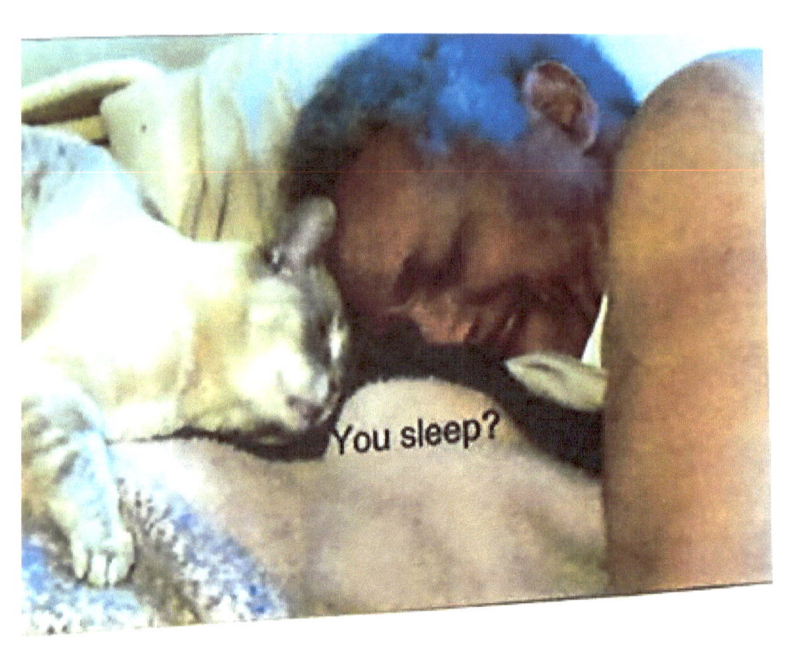

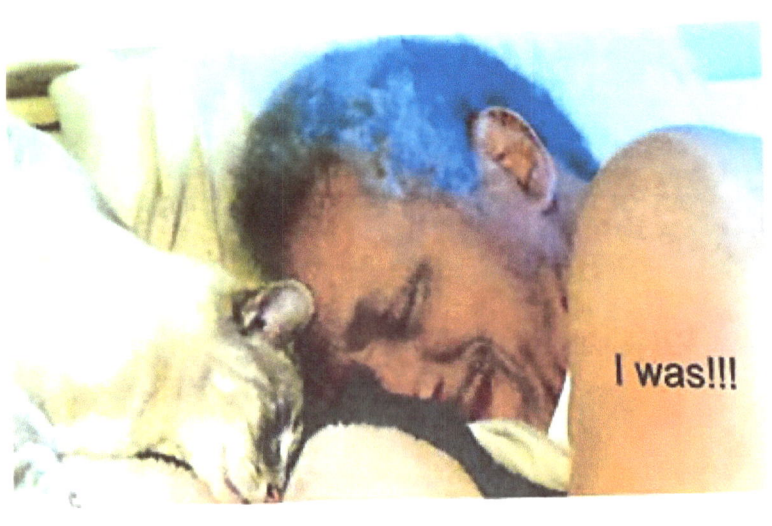

CHAPTER VIII
I NO SPEAK CAT

Shasta and I could communicate very well. But there were times when it was clear we were on different wavelengths. I could read Shasta's communiques as long as I could relate it to something that was occurring at a given moment. But there were times when, as I sat in a chair at the table, or just relaxing in some chair in the house, Shasta would walk over to me and loose a series of yowls as he looked directly at me. This would happen when I knew he wasn't hungry, the door to the outside was open and he could come or go as he chose, and he was wide awake. But I had no clue as to why he was yapping at me. I would say "What? What? What do you want?" He would stop yapping, stand there, look around, then look back to me again and start the yowling again as he stood there. I had no idea what he wanted. Soon, he would stop his yowling, gaze at me for a few more seconds, then turn and walk away and either go lay down or go outside. And each time this scenario played out and he walked away, I would have the distinct impression his thought was "how can I make him understand me"? Using my hindsight, I think he was making an urgent attempt to have a discussion with me directly, and was feeling completely frustrated because he could not make himself understood by me. Looking back at these yapping sessions, I believe they were Shasta's attempts to reverse his usual process and instead, he was trying to pull me through the door of animal awareness and into his world of feline awareness. I could read Shasta's actions and interpret his thinking, but unfortunately, I never learned "catspeak".

And that is my one regret in regard to Shasta.

FROM TIME TO TIME SHASTA WOULD TRY
TO INITIATE A DISCOURSE WITH ME...
THROUGH A SERIES OF YOWLS BUT...

I COULD NOT UNDERSTAND HIM:
UNFORTUNATELY, I NEVER LEARNED TO
SPEAK "CAT-SPEAK"

SHASTA WAS FRUSTRATED WITH ME
BECAUSE I NEVER LEARNED TO SPEAK CAT-
SPEAK

CHAPTER IX
Channeling Sumac, Not the Suez

One day I took Shasta into the vet because he was limping. I was not overly concerned, however, because over the years, various cats that I had, at some point had displayed a limp, usually the result of head-to-dead warfare with some other neighborhood feline. Sometimes, when the limp appeared quite pronounced and still obvious the second day, I would then take the cat in for treatment at some vet, such as I had done a few years previous with Shasta. Other times, when the cat with the limp was one of my strays that I fed, I simply kept an eye on it to see if the limp went away, which usually it did after two or three days. If it was one of my personal cats that developed the limp and the limp remained after two days, we would take a trip to the vet. Such was the case with Shasta. I put him in a carrying case and put it in the backseat of the car, and we headed off to the doc. He was quiet and calm as I drove. After a short period of the time on the way, there came a sound which started soft but gradually increased in volume. It took me a few seconds to realize the sound was coming from the backseat and another few seconds to realize it was coming from Shasta. Never had I ever heard such a sound from an animal before.

It started in the bass register, softly, climbed quickly, smoothly, upward, increasing in volume as it moved upward through the soprano scale, and into the higher register of the soprano scale; and then I know not if it stopped on that high not heard or if it continued into a range I could not hear. I only know that as that sound filled the car, my awareness and wonder were about 95 percent on tthat sound, leaving about five percent on my driving. I think the hairs on the back of my neck rose throughout that event. While it is true I had never heard that sound from an animal before, I had heard that sound from human before. It was in high school.

In high school, I sang on the choir which included music theory. We learned about music, singers, and instruments. We learned about a lady vocalist yma sumac, born in 1920. She was a singer with a phenomenal talent. Her vocal range encompassed about four octaves; we heard from the start on a note in the neat bass range and then run her voice up the scale in a smooth ascension into the highest soprano registry. When Shasta did was the exact same thing. It was eerie. After hearing him do that, my thoughts were was he experiencing some sort of pain or some kind of discomfort. I called out to him as I drove. He gave me an answering meow. I felt somewhat relived. We went into the exam room and I took him out of the carrying cage and set him on the examining table. He explored the top of the table then came and sat right in front of where I was standing. Usually whenever I took some one of my cats into that room, they were very nervous and tense; jumping at every sound, looking to return to the carrying cage. Shasta just sat, calmly, in from of me. The doc came in with one of his attendants. There were 4 of us in the room discussing Shasta and he remained sitting there in front of me, calmly taking it all in. Later when we were at the reception window, that attendant remarked about Shasta, "boy, we could see whose cat that is", meaning it was obvious from the way Shasta stayed in front of me and remained calm. Yes, I was special to Shasta too but to this day I have no idea what stimulated that weird vocalization. We left him there with the vet for 2 days while they ran tests, did blood work. Then they called us to come in. They told us he had cancer in his leg and that it could spread. They said his leg would have to be amputated. I was horrified! No! Not Shasta! No! But the doctor said if we did not amputate the leg, Shasta would soon die as the cancer spread. After much sad discussion, and the doctor assuring us that it was the only way, we painfully gave permission. We left him there, and that night, I cried for Shasta.

X

THE ANIMAL, THE HUMAN

I *CRIED FOR SHASTA*.

Listen. Listen and you can hear the voices start. You can hear the voices cry out, "what? Are you crazy? Are you some kind of nut? Or are you a new kind of nut? You're acting nutty about a cat? You're crying? Over a cat? Man, get a life. Get over it and get a life."

When one "gets a life", one embraces aliveness. When we accept the responsibility of having a pet, and that pet in short order becomes integral to our feeling of contentment, we then take on the life of caring for our pet's animal awareness, commit to our pet-to- human bonding, and share in the pleasure of our pet's reciprocal ownership. That is a life!

A few years ago I had a discussion with my cousin about how valuable my cat was to me. The discussion moved into encompassing anybody's feeling for his pet. Soon we set up a hypothetical scenario; a boat ride, many passengers, seas get rough. I am there with my pet. A lady, whom I don't know, is there with her young child, maybe 4 years old. A giant wave hits the boat. My pet and that lady's child is swept overboard on opposite sides of the boat. I am a strong swimmer. The lady, who can't swim screams "my baby, my baby". What would I do? Without hesitation I told my cousin i'd go after my pet. He was aghast. "You'd choose an animal over a human?" I told him there would't be a question in my mind. In that situation, the strongest pull would be for my pet, and all my energies I would throw into saving my pet. He was dumbfounded. I explained, when you have had a pet for a period of time, you develop a very strong emotional attachment to that pet, very nearly equal to what you would have for your own child.

We changed one of the objects in the hypothetical. Now it was my own child and my same pet. Again, there would be no hesitation on my part. But now it would be my own child that would be the target of all my energies. There would be an emotional attachment to both these figures, but the emotional attachment would be strongest for my own child and I would probably blank out all concern for my pet until my child was safe. My cousin felt it should be that way in any human vs animal rescue attempt. He and those who agree with him think that the rest of us are sick. They think we have some kind of disease that makes us feel the way we do about our pets, and they are right!! We do have a disease. It's called "pet-lovitus"! That's "—lovitus", with a long "I". That is "pet –love- it- us, which describes our ailment perfectly; we love our pet, and it loves us. This is a highly contagious disease, but not between humans. Humans can only catch it from their pet. The symptoms are recognizable. First you feel a smile coming on when you first look at the pet. After seeing it perform some act, you get an urge to giggle. Then you take it home, show it to your family, you all take note of its antics, and you cough up a laugh. Now if somebody points out some flaw in the pet, you feel forced to defend it. Ah-h-h-h… now you've been infected pet-lovitus and the condition will only grow deeper and deeper inside you and as the days go by, you will treat the condition with doses of attention you give to your pet every day. And when that pets' life span has run its' course and its' presence is taken from you, you won't see it as a cure but rather almost as if you kicked a habit, a powerful habit. But you haven't kicked a habit. The habit will have been ripped from you and it will be agony. And you will be left raw and bleeding where once the habit had been. And you will suffer pangs of memory and devastating symptoms of withdrawal such such as those I staggered through under the heavy, relentless, albeit spaced, pounding I absorbed at the departure of each of my pets; my nutsy, my mother, my tony, grey-boy, topsy, princess, mickey, marble, mickey, charcoal, and ten others. And then after some passage of time, and you think you have moved on, there comes a point in time when the memory faculty calls for a revisit to the departed pet and the residual effects of pet-lovitis reconnects your emotions to the eternal ethereal substance of your pet, causing those emotions to once more rise to the surface of your thinking, and you smile tears of "….If only…."… Here, let me share with you an actual scene I witnessed about 15 years ago, long before I had Shasta, a scene which is burned into my memory forever, and which demonstrates the powerful effects of this disease, pet-lovitus.

CHAPTER XI
BLACK BEAUTY, ET AL

One day about 15 years ago, I was sitting in the waiting room of a vetenarian office. I had brought another of my cats in for the doctor to attend to some minor condition he had. There were two other clients there also with their pets awaiting the vet's attention. A soft, quiet beeping floated through the room. It was akin to the soft tones one hears in a motion picture denoting the sound of an audible heart monitor. I do not know if the sound was there from the moment I entered the vet's office, or if it began after I had been there waiting. I only know I was not consciously aware of its' tones when first I entered the facility.

In a little while the front door opened and two people came in from the street and went to the receptionist's window. The woman looked to be about 25 to 35 years of age, the man about the same. They conferred with the receptionist agitatedly briefly, then waited nervously. Shortly the vet came out and spoke to them. The two people began to look quite concerned. Soon the vet left them and returned back into the confines of the hospital. After about another 10 or 15 minutes he again came out to the couple and said a few words to them. The lady began to cry and wail. The man embraced her, looking very sad. The vet tried to console them, but the lady was crying inconsolably. The man, while embracing the lady, spoke softly to the vet. The vet nodded and left. In about 5 minutes an attendant returned, carrying in his arms a beautiful, silky jet-black full-grown cat. It had a beautiful silver or gold chain around its neck. It lay limply in the attendant's arms. It was obviously deceased. When the lady saw the cat, she began to wail loudly and sob loudly. The attendant handed the cat to her. She took it ever so gently and she could not be consoled. The tears just flowed down her face as she cradled , her grey-boy, her topsy, her princess, her momma-girl, her mickey, her Bootsy, her tony, her nutsy, her mother, her Kramer, her half-pint, her marble, her lassie, her charcoal, her mother-girl, her black beauty in her arms and touched her face to his limp form. There were we 4 clients in that waiting room that day; the lady with her black beauty, which was not, because God accepted him, and we other three with our charges, which were, because we continued on with their care. Get a life? None of us knew the other three before that day. But each of us, together, had taken on the life of caring for our pets' animal awareness, committed to our pet-to-human bonding, and sharing in the pleasure of our pets' reciprocal ownership. That is a life.

After being allowed a short period to say goodby to her black beauty, the man gently removed the cat from the lady's arms, and handed it back to the attendant, who carried it back into the inner rooms of the hospital. The lady was by now crying even more loudly and more inconsolably even as the man half carried her out through the front door. She was near collapse. As the door closed behind them, you could still hear her wailing and crying as they wended their way to the parking area. Those of us still waiting in the waiting area, we three clients, were unashamedly wiping many tears from our own eyes, hurting with her. We knew! Crazy? Crying for a cat? No. It's much more than that! We all knew.

It wasn't until sometime after my own visit with the doctor that day, as I dealt with the receptionist that it clicked. That beeping sound I had noted before the lady came, was no longer audible. In fact, as I relived the sequence of events that had occurred, through her visit, I remembered that at some point the beeping had ceased and was replaced by one continuous steady monotone. That beeping had indeed been the sound of a heart monitor on the lady's cat. Now the devastating symptoms of withdrawal would begin, and our hearts went out to her.

CHAPTER XII
A NEW WAY OF WALKING

Now Shasta had undergone surgery at the vet's hospital. After 2 days they told us we could come and get him. We went there. They said the surgery went well and he was adjusting well to the missing hind leg. They brought him to us. They sat him on the exam room table. He seemed pleased to see us. HE STOOD THERE BALANCING ON his LEGS. We welcomed him, stroking him. We saw no difference in his attitude. We then took him home with us. First we turned him loose in the house so he could adjust to moving around in his most familiar surroundings. He didn't navigate perfectly at first. Operating with just 3 legs takes a bit getting used to. But we could see he was determined to overcome the problem. Later that day we allowed him to go out into the yard. His ambulatory gait consisted of him walking with his two front legs but bouncing along on his one hind leg. At times he would lose his balance. But he would immediately make another attempt at walking. It took about one day to get the hang of the right balance. All the other cats took notice of his uneven movement and would stare at him. But their staring only lasted one day. There-after they inter-acted with him the same as usual. They seemed to regard him as their big brother. They would come near him and allow him to groom them. Shasta still moved about the yard as before, but he also lay down and rested a bit more than before. After all, having only one hind leg meant his moving about called for that one leg to be working double duty, so he tired a bit more than usual. But his balancing ability improved every day. He could stand and eat, stand and drink, or just stand and survey. Shasta still liked to get on the bed and sleep whether with us or just to relax himself. But as I watched him trying to negotiate the leap up onto the bed, which he used to do with no effort, it was now a bit of a struggle. Using only one leg did not provide adequate thrust to gain proper altitude and he was left to claw his way to the level of the mattress. The same was true of the two sections of sofa in the front room. I could see this was causing him some degree of frustra-tion so i set a foot stool at these three locations; one beside each sofa section, and one at the foot of the bed. He was then able to reach the mattress level and both sofa section cushions level with-out breaking stride as he came across the floor. It was a big help to his peace of mind…and to mine.

Before his leg amputation, Shasta, like most cats, was lighting fast on his feet and agile. Now missing that leg he was less than half his fast, and his agility was nil! Consequently, out of an abundance of caution, i did not want him roaming the neighborhood as freely as had been his wont, practically the streets. Now my backyard has four points of egress available to my cats; a hole in the back fence, a hole in the front fence, a hole in the fence adjacent to one of my neighbors, and pathway up and over the fences at any point that cats can climb, Shasta, missing one leg, now found it impossible to climb over the fences. Now having sealed off the three holes in the fence, Shasta was effectivly confined to my backyard. And it was a new sense of sadness i felt, watching him move about the yard sequentially inspecting all three escape points. Moreover, i could sense his frustration at this inspection and could almost hear him giving voice to his consternation. And it hurt me to impose such a restriction on him. He loved his freedom. Of course, he could not understand this situation, but i knew keeping him away from the streets was the best way to keep him alive, given his lack of mobility.

Shasta was allowed to roam freely in the house and in the backyard. Whenever I went into the yard, I would locate him, or he would locate me, which ever of us got the first sighting. Then that one would move toward the other.

One day I went into the yard. I did not locate him, and he didn't locate and approach me. I looked around but did not see him. Thinking he was probably in the house, i went inside and looked. I didn't find him. Back to the yard, I made a more meticulous search. No Shasta! I called to him. No response. I checked the three escape holes. They were all still covered. Unease began to arise in me. Carefully, I made a thorough check of the house and then the yard, continually calling him name. No sighting, no answer, no joy. Fighting back panic i tried to think where he could be. Then it hit me. While i was in the house, the meter reader had come into the yard through the front gate and left the same way. The needle on my panic meter rose higher as i checked that gate. It was partly open. Shasta was out. The meter reader had been gone about a half hour before i missed Shasta. My panic was now fullblown. I researched the front yard. Nothing. There is a gap in the front yard fence. I went through the front yard gate. And walked the block calling his name. Nothing. I returned home and stood on the front step surveying the area on both sides of the street. Nothing! Finally, I went inside. I was extremely upset. Eventually, I forced myself to calm down. I sat down in a chair and waited and prayed, "lord, look after him please." I sat and waited, half an hour, one hour, an hour and ten minutes, and hour and a half, an hour and forty-five minutes. From time to time, i went to the door and looked out and then returned to sit and wait. Two hours, i got up, went to the front door, looked out, and was promptly hit in the face with a large dose of great joy. There, coming across my neighbor's front lawn, as fast as his hippity-hop self could move was Shasta. He came through the gap in the fence, went through the gate leading to the back which I had left open. I closed that gate and went to the backyard. He was there resting on his pillow. I picked him up, carried him into the house, and sat him down near a bowl of water. He drank. I didn't bother to ask him where he'd been. He wouldn't have told me anyway. We agreed that we would never speak of this escape. I was so relieved that he was back and okay that I pretended not to notice that contented look on his face. He had seized the opportunity for his final taste of pure freedom. He had escaped. He had gone somewhere. He spent over two hours enjoying his freedom and now...Now he was back, and he was contented. He was back, and I was beyond relieved. Enough said.

As he adjusted to life without one of his legs, his personality never changed. He remained as up-beat as usual. He continued to chase one of his lady friends, Cleo, around the yard. Although he couldn't keep up with her, he remained hopeful. He continued to be demanding. Sometimes when i slept past my usual getting up time, i would be awakened by Shasta's distinctive call, telling me to wake up and get him something to eat, or get up and let him go outside. Sometimes after responding to his wake-me-up call, I would get up and first go into the bathroom. After being in there for perhaps 5 or so minutes, i would again hear Shasta's call piercing the bathroom door, telling me I'd been in there long enough. When I'd open the door, there would be Shasta, his face perhaps 4 or 5 inches from the door opening, telling me to get with it! So what else could i say but "yes sir, Mr. Shasta."

Though one of his legs was missing, he continued to be open and accessible to the little people. One day my wife's grandchildren came to visit. Shasta was in the back yard and theyn hadn't seen him. Eventually my wife gave them coloring books so they could occupy their time. They sat down and began to be busy. Shortly, Shasta came in and seeing the kids busy, he hurried over to the sofa where one of them was busy. He used the footstool and hopped up on the sofa and settled himself right beside the child. He remained there while the child worked. Shasta was still giving of himself!

CHAPTER XIII
SHASTA'S GIFT

It was during this period that Shasta gave the first demonstration of his final foray into the arena of human awareness. Once I under-stood it, it stunned me. Because once I understood it, I recognized it as the culmination of all his previous forays, and once I understood

It i saw that he was giving me a gift. It was the most beautiful gift that he could have given me. IN THIS, HIS 7th FORAY INTO HUMAN AWARENESS, HE INITIATED AN ACTION THAT HAD MEANING AND SIGNIFICANCE IN THE ARENA OF HUMAN AWARENESS. And he did it with purpose. He did it with understanding. And when i witnessed this action, when i experienced this action and recognized it for what it was, i was amazed!!! I had often picked Shasta up and cuddled him in my arms. As i mentioned before, he wasn't crazy about this move but he tolerated it for 30 to 45 seconds, before indicating that he wanted to be put down, and always I accommodated him. One day I picked him up, cuddled him, when he did two things he'd never done before. About 5 seconds after I picked him up, he leaned his head gently against my left shoulder and at the same time he stretched his right paw for-ward and reached around behind my left bicep, just above my elbow, gently grasped my arm there and exerted a light pressure, pulling and holding my arm toward him. These two actions constituted an unmistakable gesture--he was actively embracing me!!! It took a couple of seconds for it to dawn on me what he was doing. Once it did, i was surprised! Pleasantly so. I held very still, cuddling him. We stood thus for about 5 to 8 seconds. At that point he released the slight pressure at the back of my arm, relaxed for another 5 or so seconds, then indicated he wanted to be put down.

I didn't fully grasp what had just happened until i replayed the scenario in my mind several minutes later. With understanding came a big smile. By embracing me the way he did, not in an animal way but in a human way, Shasta was telling me that thanks to our connectedness, gained through our mutual permissiveness as we both freely observed each other, he now knew how best to show the depth of his appreciation. Through connectedness he understood that a human embrace speaks wonders when one wishes to convey the depth of affection that grows out of that connectedness. He may not know the English word love, but he knew the value of that word when every action, associated with that word, delivers that word in truth. And so my Shasta, after gaining all that he had gained in his forays between the two awarenesses, desired to give the greatest gift he could to me, his Charles. With that embrace, he succeeded.

He must have sensed how extraordinarily pleased I was at this action for he repeated it on three subsequent occasions. Then again, I wonder if he realized that with that embrace he had reached the culmination of his 10 year quest, which began when kitty, thinking she was teaching Shasta a friendly gesture, butting heads, in reality, from his point of view, was actually Shasta beginning his early attempts to probe into the area of human awareness. In his innate high level of intelligence, I think he sensed that there was something beyond his feline awareness. Remember, she said when she tried this same tactic with other cats, as did I, it didn't take. The other cats' thinking had no inkling of anything about what we know as human awareness. Whenever we moved our face toward the face of the other cats, they became alarmed. Their expression said "what are you doing? Are you trying to bite me? Get away from me!"...As they frantically would rip themselves out of your presence. But when you moved your face and head toward shasta, he immediately would come forward to meet you and connect himself to you at (and i wonder if he knew?) The "thinking point"____the head___and maintained that contact for several seconds (had he seen mr. Spock's "mind meld"?). He never failed to accommodate you when you initiated this gesture. But the interesting and curious thing about this interaction is that shasta initiated it with me! I was not aware of this tactic at all before he introduced it to me. He had been with us only about 10 days and i happened to be getting acquainted with him, talking to him as he sat on our bed, when he for the first time, moved toward me and gently pressed his forehead against mine. It was a total surprise and a very pleasant experience. At the time that's all i thought it was. But now, hind sight being 20/20 i can't help but wonder if shasta was giving me his first probing as he searched for a door into human awareness.

Beginning with that moment and stretching out through 10 years, Shasta and I became connected by a strong bond, forged out of one word---special. Shasta was special to me and I was special to him.

Shasta found that door into human awareness and stepped through it seven times;

#1___touching his head to mine

#2___raising his head to contact my chin

#3___defending his brother the way he did

#4___enduring the chaos of the little people

#5___touching my face gently with his claws

#6___caressing my face with his paw, claws sheathed

#7___and finally, deliberately embracing me with his head and paw.

And as those 10 years unfolded, I was privileged to witness Shasta function in both the human awareness domain and the animal awareness domain, with a most unique demonstration of his prowess in the animal awareness domain when he performed that ritual which gave flame permission to become a part of his, Shasta's, family. With this ritual he again demonstrated his willingness to risk his own safety, exposing his throat to flame in order to accomplish a connection he deemed worthy. This cat was special!!

CHAPTER XIV
WE TWO

Cats are notorious for claiming, maintaining, and demonstrating their independence. It is a badge of their dignity, and they guard it ferociously. It is their credential, the permit that gives them credibility in the feline universe. No self-respecting feline would ever admit that they needed permission to function in any capacity, travel to any location, trespass any area or seek the approval or attention of a human. This propensity was bequeathed them by God almighty when he brought forth the beasts of the field and no self-respecting feline would deign to allow a human to lay claim to altering that feline intention, direction, much less appear to warrant that feline attention.....Or.....Would it??

During the period of his missing leg, sometimes when I would go out the back door heading for the garage, I would look to my left where I would see Shasta relaxing in the open-faced cabinet against the fence. He would be looking at me. As soon as I looked at him he would get himself up and quickly hop in my direction on a path that would intercept my path. When he was within about 2 feet of me, he would gently lay down on his side and wait for me to begin stroking him as he lay there. I would pet his entire body, and he was pleased by that. He would stretch and preen in the warm sunlight. Often as soon as i would begin petting him, other cats would come for me to pet them as well, which i would do, but Shasta would get most of my attention. The other cats, bug, a twin, Cleo, would rub against Shasta and he would groom whichever cat asked for it.

Many times Shasta would stretch out on his side on the grass in the warm sunlight, and look to me to come stroke him. He seemed to like that very much. Most of the time on warm days, the other cats would seek shelter from the sun. But Shasta seemed to like the warmth of the sun and would just lay there sunning himself. Sometimes when he would flop down waiting for me to begin stroking him, he would begin grooming himself, licking his paw and wiping his face. I always began petting him as soon as he lay down. But sometimes just to see what he would do, i would deliberately delay before petting him. In a few seconds he would realize that i was not accommodating him and he would pause in his ablution, raise his head and (i could swear he would have one eye closed) look at me as if to say "well? "Meaning "what are you waiting for, an invitation?" I would laugh, reach down and do my duty. Him? He would just stretch out and receive my touch, looking very contented. Yes, he was telling me i was special to him too.

CHAPTER XV
THREE QUESTIONS

A few weeks later...

Shasta had stopped eating for two days. He also was having difficulty trying to have bowel movements. On the third day, Tuesday, I didn't see him drink water, so we took him to the vet to be examined. After examining him they said he was dehydrated, and they needed to keep him overnight. We left him there. The next day, Wednesday, we went back. We didn't see him but the doc talked to us and said some of his internal organs were not functioning as they should and they needed to keep him overnight again and perform further tests. We left him there and returned the next morning, Thursday, at which time the doc informed us that his condition was hopeless and we should consider having him put to sleep soon!. This news was devastating to us, to say the least. We asked them to bring him to us, which they did. He was agitated and disoriented and didn't seem to focus on anything, just kept meowing and turning from side to side. I picked him up and kept talking to him as I held him. He kept twisting from side to side, meowing, his face turning left, right, left. This continued for several minutes. But then, suddenly he brought his face around and stopped, his gaze fastened onto my face and he was calmly, quietly, looking straight into my eyes, not moving, focusing on my face. I believe he was processing the bridging of that wall to human awareness. His mind was working and making the connections which brought him into human awareness. He was giving up all claim to his rights to feline independence. He was abandoning all pretense of feline indifference, and instead was opening up direct lines of communication. He poured all of himself into that look. He was giving me a clear, unequivocal message.

After having been around Shasta for 10 years, knowing him, watching him, observing him for those ten years, my imagination believes it knows what he was thinking. His look was saying"...do you remember when I..." and I said " yes Shasta, I remember. You almost got hit that day". He smiled. Then he said, "and do you remember when you were washing the dishes…" I said "you broke two glasses that day". He smiled. I said "and then there was that grey cat you chased…" he said "I caught him and he almost killed me!" We both laughed. We exchanged 10 years of memories in that 15-20 seconds of eye contact. Finally, he said "Charles, thank you for giving me 10 years of real love". And I said "Shasta, thank you for giving me 10 years of real love". Then, as he continued to look into my eyes, not moving, knowing his body was failing, his eyes asked me 3 questions. They were saying;

1. "Charles, you understand, don't you?" My eyes answered "yes Shasta, I understand." And he said "good". Then his eyes said

2. "Charles, I understand don't I?" And my eyes answered "yes Shasta, you do understand". And he said "good". He paused a moment, then his eyes said,

3. "Charles, I made the connection didn't i?" My eyes answered "yes Shasta, you made the connection". His eyes smiled, and he said "good". A few seconds later he lost focus and became agitated again. I continued to say "I'm here Shasta, I'm here boy" as I held him, trying to give him as much comfort as i could. Throughout the period of his agitation, my wife and I agonized over the thought of giving the doctor the O.K. To put Shasta to sleep. We didn't want him to suffer needlessly. The thought of saying goodby was devastating. We had brought Shasta into this place 3 days before. For 3 days he had been probed, handled by strangers, endured intrusive examinations, lacking the comforts of his home, missing the closeness of his feline family. For three days he had been without the loving touch of the two humans who loved him the most and now, after 3 days of enduring all this, he now was to be abandoned into oblivion????

No!!!!! After consulting with the doctor who assured us that the pain medication would hold him for another day, we decided to take Shasta home with us. Even before we made that decision, Shasta had begun to calm down. He began to focus on things a bit better than he had earlier in this visit. Once we got him home and turned him loose in his own stomping grounds, he became more relaxed. His family welcomed him back with body rubs and grooming.

He moved about the familiar surroundings as always. At one point, after he had stretched out on the sofa, dozing, i went over to him and began to gently stroke his side. I was rewarded. I was rewarded by the feel and quiet sound of Shasta purring! That gave me unimaginable joy. It was rare when I heard Shasta purr. For me this was a great sign of confirmation that we had done the right thing. The 3 questions he had asked?

Question #1….he asked did I understand that he was cognizant of the two awarenesses. I answered "yes"

Question#2….he asked was he accurate in his perception of the two awarenesses. I answered "yes Shasta, you were right on".

Question#3….he asked "Charles, I made the connection didn't I? Though I am an animal and have animal awareness, was I successful in functioning within human awareness in a manner that was pleasing and acceptable to you humans?" And I answered "oh yes Shasta, you did, you definitely did. You connected animal awareness to human awareness, and you connected human awareness to animal awareness, and every human that met you recognized that you are special!" His eyes smiled and he said "good"

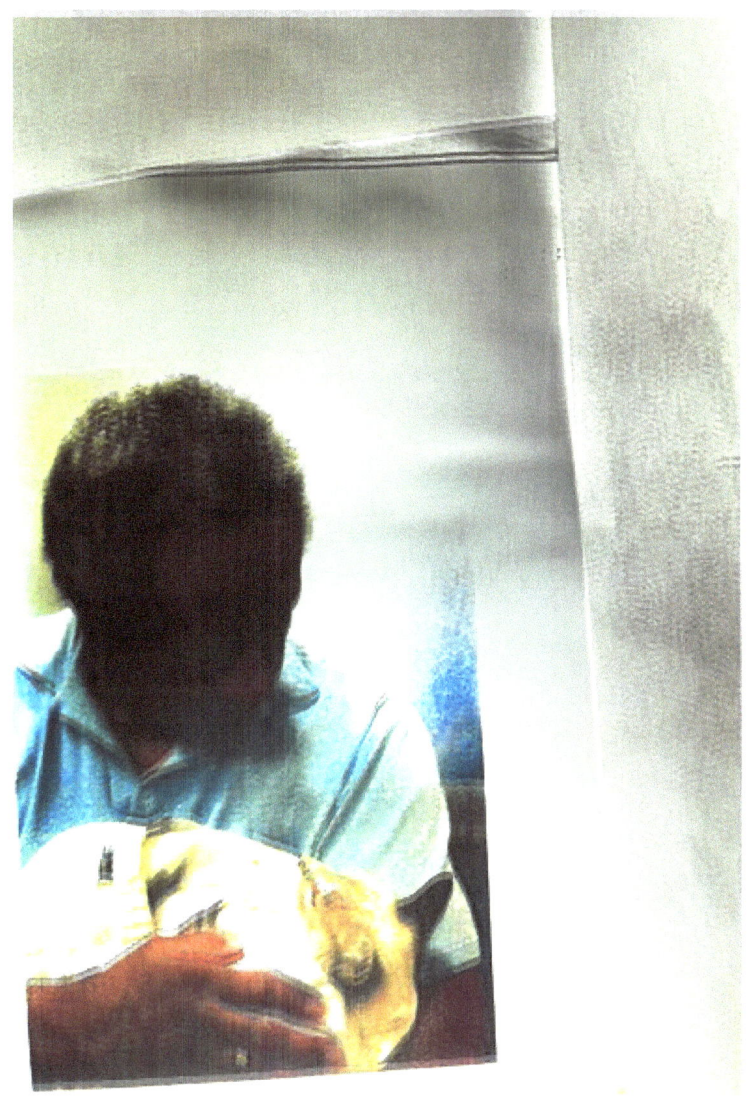

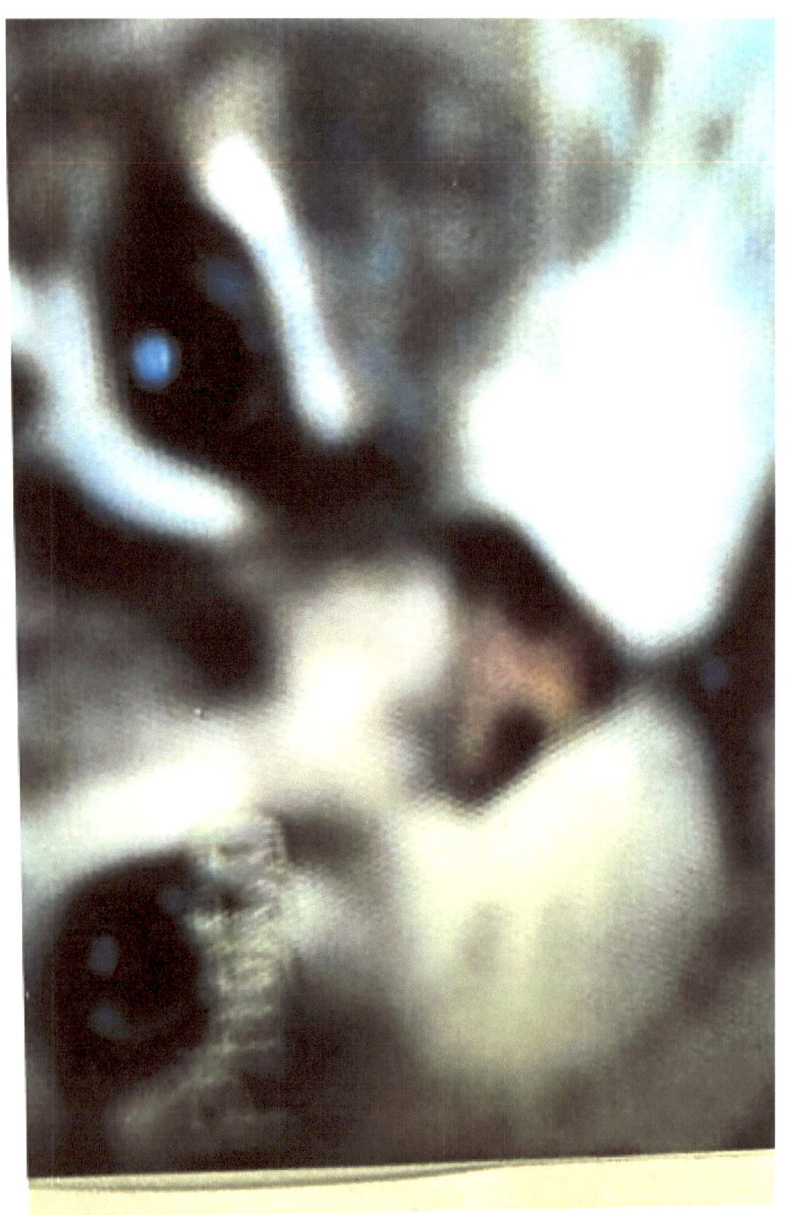

CHAPTER XVI

HUSH

The next morning, Friday, I awoke early and got up. This was to be our last morning with him. I showered, got dressed in my sweats, went into the front room. We had let Shasta relax in the carrier on warm blankets with the carrier door open. He was there now, awake. I wanted to spend as much time as i could with him this morning before we had to take him back to the vet this last time. I laid down on my exercise mat near his carrier. He started to come out to join me but paused, then retreated. I was a little puzzled by this action. But after a little thought, I figured it out. Now that he only has three legs, Shasta finds it necessary to rest a lot when in the back yard. He laid claim to a couch pillow out there and could often be seen reclining on that pillow.

I hurried out to the back yard, retrieved that pillow, brought it back into the front room and put that pillow on the floor near his carrier as soon as he saw that pillow, he immediately came out of the carrier and scurried over to that pillow, climbed up on it, and relaxed. I lay there on my mat just looking at him. He, for his part, was not looking at me. Instead, he spent the time gazing first in one direction and then the other. Occasionally, his gaze would touch my face, hold for a few seconds, then move on to some other point, and hold there. He was quiet. I was quiet, each of us valuing the nearness of the other. It was as if he was using these precious final last moments together to quietly evaluate and access those things he spent his life learning. Probably he was assessing this, eliminating that, embracing these items, throwing out those, finding contentment with what he, living his life, had learned. We did not speak...there was no need.

All to soon, the hour of our departure arrived.

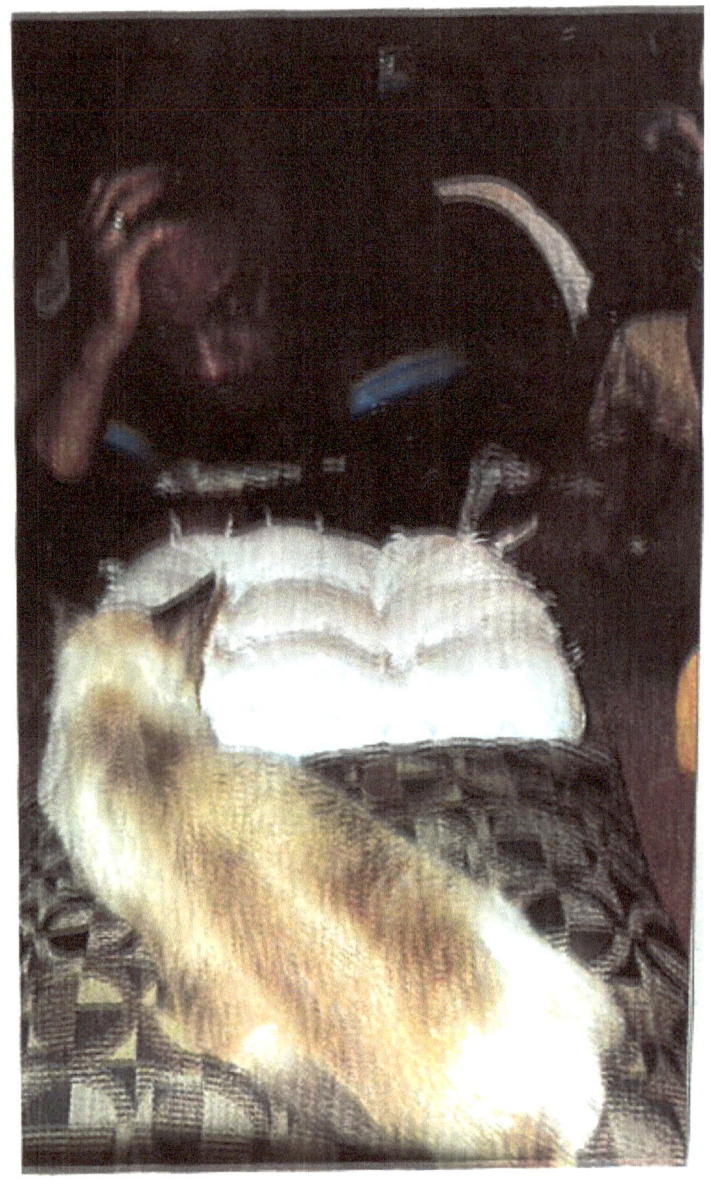

CHAPTER XVII
WE THREE

We left home that Friday morning, taking him for the last time to the vet. He was to be put to sleep. His condition was hopeless. I carried him in my lap on a cushion. I didn't want his last ride to be in a cold cage. Ellie drove. On the way there he was at times calm, then at times highly agitated. We arrived at the vet and i carried him in. They put us in a room. They let us have some time alone with him. I held him, talked to him, tried to calm him through my tears. He continued in turn calm, then agitated. Ellie took him, to hold him. It was the same. Finally she gave him back to me and left the room. Later she told me that as she held him, she told him "I love you, Shasta" he then looked at her for a moment and she said his look was telling her that he loved her too. She said his look also said that he wished "to be alone with Charles".

After Ellie left out of the room and as I held Shasta, I understood that the 3 questions he had asked me with his eyes embodied this truth which he wanted me to know; "Charles, I entrusted you to witness my efforts which defined my presence. Now I am entrusting you to share my presence with those who can understand".

That I will do.

Soon my wife returned. We took last pictures of him. He grew calmer. I laid him on the cushion we had come with. He was quiet. It was as if he knew what was coming and was accepting it. Soon the doctor came in. Soon the needle came in. Shortly there-after, Shasta left, but shortly before he left, the last thing he said to me, as he delayed the slowly closing window of animal-to human-to animal awareness was "Charles, don't forget me". I told him "No Shasta, I won't forget you. I'll never forget you".

After a little while my wife and I left.

So now, to those of you who can understand, to you, in this writing, i speak for Shasta. Shasta is gone. I'll never see him again. But he lives in my photos, in my mind, in my memory, in my thoughts, in my heart. I speak for Shasta. Domesticated cats, by species, are small and stature. Shasta, as he loved his life, projected a present much, much larger than himself, and all though he is gone now, his presence remains and, from time to time, eases itself into my awareness, like a...cat.

Don't forget me

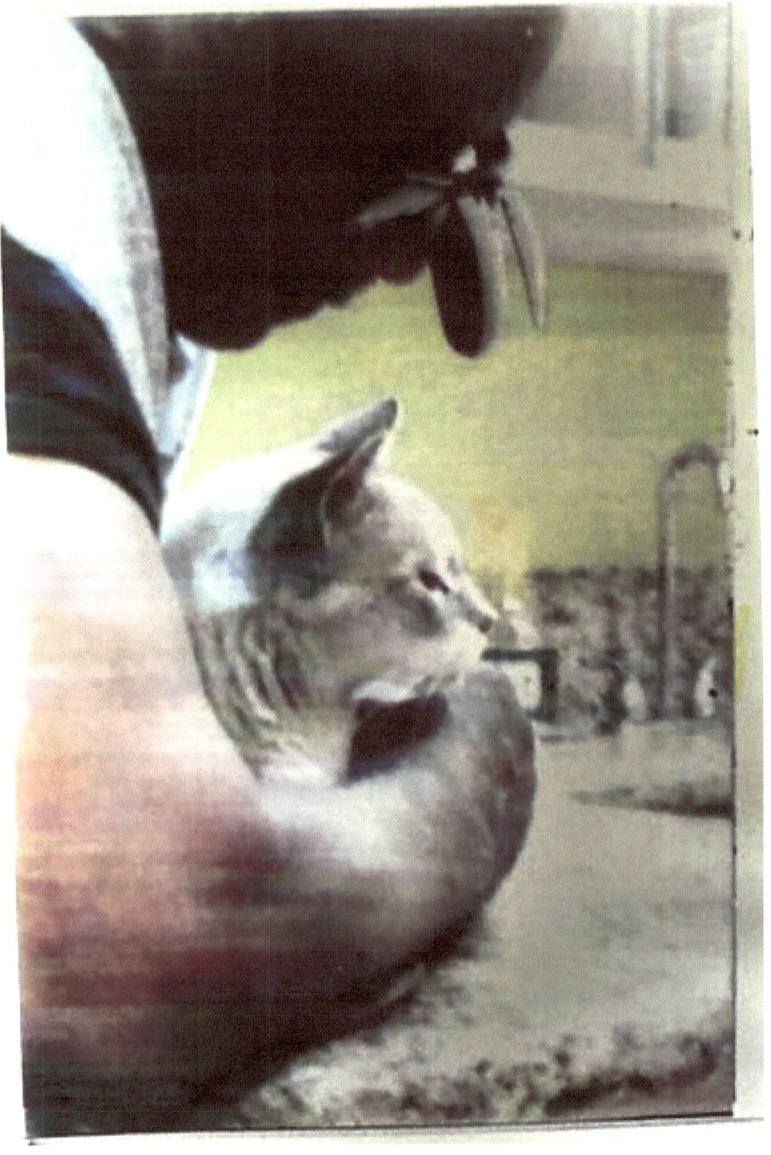

I love you Shasta

PART 3: DICHOTOMY

CHAPTER 1

Everything seemed so hazy now. It was as if he were coming out of a fog. What had happened? It wasn't yet quite clear but…..Seems like….. Then it all flooded back____the fire! The fire! Everything burning! The animals panicing! Everybody running. It was horrible!

The men came and fought the fire. It took them some time to control it but they got it out. That was a long time ago. He lost so many friends and neighbors. He lost his family. A long time ago…..Long time ago. And still the smell of smoke and burning buildings hung in the air. It had even clung to him for a while…for a long while.

The year of the fire he was just a youngster, living on the farm…. Farm…oh, now that's right. He lived on a farm, and it was the farm that was burning.

The farm was the only home he had ever known. He was raised there. But now the fire had destroyed everything, his neighborhood, his family, his home. Now he was homeless.

He hated fire. He feared fire. He remembers, after the fire, being carried to a large grey building. There he was reunited with some of his neighbors and many of them looked quite fatigued____like they'd been through hell. Well, it was a fire after all.

They left him here with his neighbors for a time. He new he was going to have to wait his turn. He watched as they worked with his friends, determining which ones were seriously injured and which ones were not. They sent some to one section, others to another. Several of them were too far gone to save. These were transferred to another grey building. He never saw them again.

But here he can speak for himself, listen to him.

"And then there was the old guy. Everybody knew the old guy. He was the oldest in our neighborhood. Nobody seemed to know when it was he came to our neighborhood.It seems like when each of us came to the neighborhood he was already there.All of us kind of looked up to him. He was our role model. Now he too had been injured in the fire. He had some smoke damage and burns. Still he was triing to stand. I think he was triing to set an example for the rest of us.

Finally they came to look me over. They gave me a complete physical from head to feet. Later they tried to get me to stand, but i just sort of toppled over, which surprised me. I thought i was stronger than that.

So they looked me over a little closer. I never was one to say much. They fed me, gave me a lot of water. They said i'd be back in shape again in no time. After all, i was young, and strong, and tall"

CHAPTER II

The sign said "visitors welcome". Over time he began to see a number of people passing through, sometimes groups, sometimes couples, sometimes singles. Many came into where he was. They asked about him, looked him over while he just stood there. They touched him, asked questions about him. They were told his background. Often some got so far as to discuss taking him with them. But usually that's as far as it went.

As they would inquire of him, he would always observe them. The blonde was nice. The older couple were funny. The hispanic couple were about to decide but something changed their mind. The mixed couple also were about set but then the wife had an attack of vertigo and they had to leave abruptly.

It was just before the jewish couple came through that he saw his first one. It came in quietly. The jewish couple passed on through soon after, the couple with the three kids appeared. They had been here before, the two adults, but without the three kids. Now they were back with the kids. While the two adults held a discussion with the lady who had brought them to him, they were touching him and laughing. Finally the man said "well what do you think kids?" And all three kids said "yes!"

CHAPTER III

They completed the paper work, the man signed it and soon thereafter, he found himself joining them on their ride home. They pulled into their garage and everybody climbed out. They embraced him all the way inside. He felt warm all over. He felt good. No longer was he homeless. It was a three bedroom house, two baths. A den, patio, front room. There was plenty of room. He wouldn"t be cramped. He fit right in.

CHAPTER IV

He had been with this family for almost two weeks when he spotted the tenth one from time to time he would see them.

He had been hearing much conversation about the coming gathering of many folk, family, friends, relatives. It was to be a reunion. Up 'til now the activities of the several family members concerned each of them separately. But now, as the time of the reunion drew closer, the focus of the household activities began to narrow in one direction. The daily discussions of neighborhood, city, and state events were now tinged with laughter and frivolity. This was a happy family. He felt lucky and priviledged to have been accepted into it. Even their pet parakeet accepted him. At first it kept

Its distance. But he'd been here for awhile now and the bird had begun to warm up to him, had grown comfortable around him. It would light on his head or one of his arms, or foot.

As they spoke of the coming reunion, they could see that this was all a new thing to him. Then number 18 showed up. They seemed to be coming faster now.

As they began to plan for the reunion, the little kids began to offer suggestions that he saw were aimed at making sure he got the full impact of this family event that was coming down the track. They also spoke of cooking and baking and drinking, of music and dancing and singing. During the period of time he had been with this family he had marveled at the way they always pitched in together to accomplish whatever task was set before them. It didn't matter whether it was the adults' task or children's task. Each member contributed his part.

Now they turned their attention on him. Hr was wearing the same outfit he had arrived in. He often wore it but it was kept clean. Now they said he was going to get dressed like he had never dressed before.

Finally they all stepped back to give him room. Judging from the smiles on their faces, he knew he was making them proud. When he saw himself in the mirror on the other side of the room, he seconded the emotion. He was more than well pleased. Dressed in his new outfit, he almost didn't recognize himself. From top t o bottom he was a sight to behold. Bring on that reunion 'cause he was ready.

CHAPTER V

At last the day arrived. All along he had been feeling the family's pent—up anticipation which, with each passing day had been becoming more difficult to hold back. But now, finally there was no longer a need for restraint. The children had planned to be first up. But they were too slow. He was already up. They were second. Now the entire family had come alive and the tension was palpable, so much so that his whole being was quivering with excitement. The reunion was on. From mid-morning on, people were continually coming and going, mostly staying. And what's more, without fail, all who entered acknowledged him and favored him with a smile and would remark how good he looked. He was so happy he could just spit.

Now the house was nearly bursting with people. In his short, young life, he had never been held in such high esteem. His life on the farm had been ordinary, quiet, even mundane. But now he felt like a king. The whole was bright, shiny, like a brand new toy. He was so happy his face lit up with the brightness of a star. He was bursting with joy. Everybody seemed to be boiling over with joy. By mid-afternoon everybody was bursting with food. A little while later the eating stopped, and the singing began. Once more he thought this was a happy family he found himself in. They loved to sing. They had this little game they'd play. They asked each other what their favorite song was, and then they would all sing it. Then they'd ask another member and they would all sing that one. He had never experianced this joyful practice before. He didn't have a favorite tune. No mater. They would just sing a song about him.   Man, that was great. Now, here at the reunion this practice was magnified ten fold.

CHAPTER VI

They came down the stairs. First one, then another, 'til the whole family was up and about. Good mornings were tossed about freely, happily. He stood there, arms outstretched, ready to receive their god mornings and their embraces. The children were still as happy and excited as could be about yesterday's reunion. The adults were also still happy but their excitement level was not as high today as it had been the previous day. Everyone seemed to be so busy this day, coming and going, other family members and friends dropping by, none giving him much more than a cursory glance. Still he remained calm and quiet. As he looked around he wondered what could have caused such a change from near praise yesterday to near disdain today? What had he said? What had he done? Yesterday they embraced him. Today they barely glance at him. Yesterday they all seemed to want to be near him. Today they seem to want to avoid being anywhere in his vicinity. He thought "what, have i become invisible?" The outfit they had so laboriously help dress him in a short while ago, that he wore so proudly, now seemed to weigh on him heavily. In fact he was beginning to not feel so proud. Where-as a little while ago, about when he saw the twenty fourth one, he stood up straight and tall, proud to be part of this family, he now was feeling weary, less proud. His shoulders were beginning to droop.

It had never been his nature to create a commotion, but now he gathered himself, trembling with suppressed rage, he shook off the stupor brought on by benign neglect and screamed into the house "not too long ago ('about when i saw #25' he thought) i was the center of attention. Now it's as if i'm the center of the hole in the center of the earth! What's going on here?" But no one answered him.

Suddenly he saw the 27th one moving quickly. The memory of the fire flashed across his consciousness. It was so sudden and unexpected it left him numb with shock. Fire? What fire? It took a moment. Oh___ of course. The fire on the farm. But that was a while back. He'd almost forgotten. Why was that memory re-visiting him? He was quiet for a moment, nervously quiet. And then it hit him. That was when he was made to realize he was homeless___and worse___an orphan. At the time of the fire that realization caused him great consternation, and that feeling was starting to creep back into his beeing again. That same feeling, only worse__the feeling of loneliness, desolation, rejection, abandonment. The pain all this caused was so, so sharp it cut him deep, to his core even. Few have experienced the totally devestating, searing pain such as he ws feeling right now. No____no that's not quite right. Many have had this exact same calamitous emotion. It comes when one realizes they're being engulfed by cold, hard hearted rejection or worse, indifference. Sometimes, in our humanness, we csn be so hurtful without meaning to be. Sometimes we do damage unknowingly, without intent, usually through ignorance. But the pain thus caused is no less real to the recipient.

CHAPTER VII

Half asleep, he watched as the 31st one swiftly approached. He awoke to the sensation of gentle pulling and tugging. At first he was startled. But as full wakefulness crawled through his awareness, he began to realize that it was the family tugging at him. Joyfully he reached for them, playfully tugging at their clothes. They would lift his fingers from their sweaters, or shirts or blouse or cap. Their touch now wasn't as caressing as it had been when they helped him dress a few days ago. Suddenly it dawned on him. They were undressing him! They were taking back the outfit

They had bought for him. He was petrified with disbelief. "These are my togs" he mumbled. "You gave them to me". They ignored him. His struggle was feeble and brief, for he was weak from hunger and thirst. His protestations went unheard. Finally he stood there, wobbly and off balance. Instinctively he knew what was coming next. Horrified, he found himself on the street, again. Homeless, again. But these were nice people.

He sat on the curb. He was really thirsty. And he was somewhat stunned at the sudden change in his status. It left him immobilized, not even wanting to move. Where could he go? What could he do? After awhile he heard a rumbling noise. He looked up and saw a large green truck coming along the block. As he watched, he saw several of his old friends from the old neighborhood jump on board as the truck approached. When it got to him, he decided he too would hitch a ride. So he jumped___that is he tried to jump on board. Weak from lack of food and water, he needed help getting into the truck. He settled in as the truck rumbled on out of the city.

CHAPTER VIII....
(Here, i'll let him tell it)

"It was a long ride, and i was so thirsty. Finally it slowed, stopped, moved again. Each time it stopped, some of my friends jumped off. This was repeated a few times until it was my turn to jump off. So i did. I tripped and rolled down a hill. I came to rest at the bottom of the hill among acquaintances. They were stirring around. Some sat up, some sat down. Some just lay there. I could hear their soft murmuring. What were they saying? Gradually my hearing became atuned to their sounds. I could feel myself smiling. Ah___that's what it is. Each of them was taking his turn at telling the rest of us his story, where they had been, who they saw, what they saw. Many of us had been with families. Some had gotten jobs in diverse and auspicious places like city halls, hotels, train stations, airports,

Even concert halls and schools. You name it, we were there. But the homes, such as my location, were the best assignments.

Then it was my turn to share. I told them of the fire on the farm, of being homeless. I told of the great family that took me in, of the singing and the laughter, of the reunion. I told them how after the reunion the atmosphere had sort of deflated. But even as i was telling them all this, i began to see the big picture; the time i had spent with this family was, all in all, a very positive moment in time. As i concluded my account, i could see that everyone was quietly nodding in affirmation.

"And then in short order, another took the floor___or ground as it were, and began to relate his story. And as i listened to each one sharing his adventure with the group, it occurred to me that this too was a reunion and this reunion showed that no matter what the venue in which we found ourselves, we each had brought joy into focus, though only for a brief moment in time."

Man! Was he thirsty. He looked up just in time to see the thirty first one pass by. Now they were all gone. They were all used up.

He began to weep, and his pine needles began to fall off. His tears though, were bitter—sweet tears, for he knew that he had done all that he had been raised to do.

In time he stopped his weeping. He shook himself, brushed himself off with a light breeze. He looked around and saw his cousin. He smiled, leaned over and whispered.. "Happy new year, sapling".

THE END

Charles A. Faulkner

.....HEAR THE ALIVENESS

Maybe not with a tree. But surely with humans and with pets, every true relationship should have a value that lasts.

- The author

ABOUT THE AUTHOR

It was at birth that fortune first smiled on the author. For it was the mother that gave him birth that lit the fire which, in due course, grew into a conflagration which morphed into a penchant. The fire? Reading. That mother fed the fire by reading Fairey Tales and Nursery Rhymes to the author and encouraged him to participate for himself. As time passed, the author graduated to reading comic books which he devoured voraciously. About that same period his mother, who was a pianist, introduced him to music which he took to gladly. Years later that led to another penchant, composing. He has composed 1 classical piece, 2 jazz pieces, 1 soliloque-like ballad, and 6 selections for church which includes a musical drama entitled " THE TIGHTROPE". It has 4 acts, a prologue and an epilogue. The author wrote the story and the complete dialogue, but he did not write the musical selections. Instead he selected selections already written and used them in the story as the dialogue called for them. He presented the drama in his church and it was well received. In fact his choir presented him with a plaque to commemorate the occasion.

While in the military the author found himself stationed at a particular location. He had promised some civilian friends at his previous location he would write and share his impressions of this new location.

After spending a few months observing, the author, with tongue firmly planted in cheek, composed a fourteen-verse poem describing his environs. It too was well received. In fact his fellow airmen liked it so much, many of them requested and received a copy. The title? "PARADISE MISPLACED"

www.ingramcontent.com/pod-product-compliance
Lightning Source LLC
Chambersburg PA
CBHW051838140626
46547CB00023BC/68